BELIEF, FAITH AND REDEMPTION

by

RALPH A. GALLAGHER

SCHMUL PUBLISHING CO.
SCHMUL'S WESLEYAN BOOK CLUB   SALEM, OHIO

Published by Schmul Publishing Co.
PO Box 716
Salem, Ohio USA

Printed in the United States of America

ISBN 0-88019-452-9

Contents

Chapter 1

The Nature of Belief

Any attempt to work out the relationship between belief and faith is certain to be difficult. The mind is so fluid that it is not easy to draw the boundaries between the various mental states and activities. Our problem is made more difficult because we have the habit of using belief and faith as synonymous terms. This confusion of terms is not conducive to clear perceptions and understanding. It is to be hoped that the Lord depends more upon our thoughts and intents than upon our verbalizations. It will be the basic assumption of this study that belief and faith are different in character and activity. Belief must always precede faith.

Beliefs are acquired; they are not standard equipment of the mental life. Faith is standard equipment of the mental life. God has given to every man a measure of faith (Romans 12:3). The belief-faith sequence is hearing—hope—reason—belief—faith—experience—knowledge. We cannot say how early in life the human mind begins to acquire beliefs. Does the infant establish the belief that if it cries it will be fed? We have no way of knowing. The beliefs that concern us are those that are developed later in life.

Many beliefs are acquired from parents and others around us in childhood days. These are not the result of a more or less lengthy process of reasoning but are accepted on the basis of authority. As we grow older, the process of establishing our own beliefs develop.

Beliefs may be simple or complex. They may involve a single idea or they involve a world view. The year 1492 A.D. is a relatively simple idea. But the belief that it was an important year will require considerable thought to establish that fact. Historical facts such as Columbus' discovery of America, etc. would have to be cited as proof.

Charles S. Peirce believed that the sole function of thought was to establish our beliefs (Charles S. Peirce: *Selected Writings*, p. 118). We may define belief "as our fixed attitude toward that which we accept as true." Beliefs may be adopted as principles by which we direct our lives. They guide our desires and shape our actions (*Ibid.*, p. 98). Beliefs have the nature of habits (*Ibid.*, p. 101). The essence of belief is the establishment of habit, and different beliefs are distinguished by different modes of actions to which they give rise (*Ibid.*, p. 121). In other words, some beliefs may become principles upon which we are willing to act.

A belief may light the fires of hope that send a light far down future's broadening way. Man's greatest hope and search has been for an assured way to eternal life. Words cannot portray an adequate picture of man's strivings to satisfy this hope of a continuing life after death. These efforts have ranged from the grossest indulgence of the fleshly appetites, the burning of their children as sacrifices upon the altars of their gods, to the loftiest and noblest flights of the imagination of the most refined minds.

Belief is a very elastic word. It may include a very simple idea or it may be expanded to a life style or even a world view. In spite of its elasticity it cannot be stretched to cover the least of that which we regard as untrue. Belief cannot transform untruth into truth. Nor is belief a guarantee that the thing believed is true. We "believe" ourselves into heaven and we "believe" ourselves into hell. The responsibility is ours. The mature adult mind chooses the beliefs that it wishes to adopt as principles to live by.

Our beliefs are of vital importance. The ends to which they lead are predestined. Some beliefs lead to an eternity with God, and some lead to an eternity without God. It is possible to adopt a belief that is not true. The Bible does speak of those that God sends a strong delusion that they may believe a lie "that they all might be damned who believe not the truth" (II Thess. 2:10-12). This Scripture applies in a special way to the end times, but we cannot help but wonder if God has been using this procedure in all ages. At least our beliefs should be carefully thought out and adopted with fear and trembling.

Beliefs are important because they may become objects of our faith. As long as they remain mere beliefs, they have little or no impact upon us. Not all beliefs are of equal importance to us. It is a common belief that a college education is desirable. But this belief is more important to some than it is to others. Those that desire to spend their lives "digging ditches" feel no urge to attend college. Others who desire to become professionals feel that a college education is a "must" for them.

Now a college education is not something that you go down to the corner store and buy today or tomorrow. It means several years of hard work and it requires a fairly high degree of ability. It also costs a lot of money. Young people must assess their ability to meet all that a college education demands. At this stage they cannot see all that may transpire in the next few years. If they believe that they can meet every demand that may arise, they commit themselves to the venture and register at the college of their choice. Their belief in a college education has now become an object of their faith. They have not committed themselves not only to seeking a college education, but they have also committed themselves to whatever the object of their faith may demand of them. These demands will unfold as the days pass by. There will be the "expected" and the "unexpected."

This willingness to launch out in pursuit of a future goal is what we call faith. This kind of faith is standard equipment for human minds. The little child manifests this faith when it accepts its father's promise to bring it a bag of candy from the store. This is the faith that we exercise every day of our lives.

CHAPTER 2

The Nature of Faith

Our search for the true nature of faith will involve the stripping off of a considerable over-burden before we reach the pure vein we are seeking. The broad generalized use of the word faith adds to the obscurity of its true nature and meaning. (1) Many times it refers to a system of doctrines which we call a creed. (2) Faith may also be thought of as that which relates us to God. At the best, this is usually a very vague concept. (3) A common concept is that faith is a means of obtaining things from God. This expresses the instrumental aspect of faith and does, I think, point in the direction of the true nature of faith.

Too often the wordy discussions of faith do more to obscure than to throw light upon its nature. This is especially true in regards to its relation to reason. Generally, the aim in such discussions is to prove that one is superior to the other. This sort of debate is a waste of time. We must always keep in mind that faith and reason are but two facts of the mind or personality. Reason has to do with (1) the process of the establishment of truth. (2) It has to do with the determination of choice when several options are present. For the purpose of analytical study it is acceptable procedure to abstract them from the whole mind or personality. But we must always keep in mind that they are abstractions. Failure to do this will result in a logical fallacy that Professor Whitehead called misplaced concreteness. This in turn leads to confusion. The part is confused for the whole.

At the present time, some say, we are in the midst of a revolt against reason. Faith and emotion (sentiment or matters of the heart) are exalted above reason. We are told that this is a backlash from the overemphasis of reason in science. This may be true, we do have a habit of pursuing a pendulum course. It must be continually borne in mind that in the case of faith and reason it is not an either-or situation. There is no hostility or conflict between faith and reason when they are understood and properly related. What God has joined together, let not man put asunder!

Our concept of faith is still suffering from medieval accretions. During that period faith was exalted at the expense of reason. Reason took a terrible beating. Martin Luther's view of reason was probably somewhat typical. He said,

> That silly little fool, that Devil's bride, Dame Reason, God's worst enemy. We know that reason is the Devil's harlot, and can do nothing but slander and harm all that God says or does. If, outside of Christ, you wish by your own thought to know your relation to God, you will break your neck. Thunder strikes him who examines. It is Satan's wisdom to tell what God is, and by doing so he will drag you into the abyss. Therefore keep to Revelation and do not try to understand. (Randall, *The Making of the Modern Mind*)

It would seem that Dr. Luther got carried away by his oratory!

The medieval mind separated faith so far from reason that faith became little more than fanaticism and superstition. The more incredible a proposition was, the more merit there was in believing it. This was a very distorted situation and it falls far short of the Biblical concept of faith. It could be that this misunderstanding of faith and reason has helped to generate some of the conflict between science and religion. Some of this misty medieval garb still clings to our concept of faith.

An error that may be a handicap in understanding faith is the notion that it is mainly a matter of religion. This is far from the truth. We live, move, and have our being, so to speak, in faith. It is as common to all men as the air we breathe. Human enterprises would be impossible without faith. The whole scientific endeavor would break down if faith were lacking. Every scientist must exercise faith in his methodology. We cannot avoid exercising faith.

Many attempts have been made to define faith. Let us now look at several of these.

1. "The category of despair"—A melancholy Dane.
2. A "Leap in the dark"—Existentialism.
3. "It is an empty hand reaching out to God"—Anon.
4. "A venture dictated by human interest"—Tennant.

5. "Faith is the creative power in man"—Unamuno.

6. "Faith is the total assent of a man's total being to Jesus Christ"—Barclay.

7. "Faith is the state of being ultimately concerned" —Tillich.

8. "Faith is the vision of the ideal and affirmation and the discovery of spirit that this vision is ultimately true" —Ferre.

9. "Faith is but a whole-hearted trust in God's word as true"—Carnell.

10. "Faith is conviction apart from or in excess of proof" —Anon.

11. "Faith is a shivering, naked apprehension" —Collingwood.

12. "Faith is a heartfelt confidence and trust in the mercy of God"—Luther.

13. "Now faith is the substance of things hoped for, the evidence of things not seen"—Bible.

Such a list suggests that faith is very complex and that it is not easy to define or describe. This is certainly true. But we do find that definitions are helpful. A considerable study of faith could be developed from the above list. However, it is not within the present scope of this study to make such an attempt.

A number of years ago, in preparing a chapel message, I needed a definition of faith—a definition that would reflect the dynamic character of faith. In its most recent version it goes like this—"Faith is believing and acting upon that which is not yet present to the senses." I believe this conforms to the Biblical concept of faith.

Several things need to be said about this definition. It is a general description of faith. It applies to the secular as well as the religious areas of life. It meets the requirements of faith as set forth in Hebrews 11:6. (a) It originates with a belief in God. (b) There is a commitment to and a pursuit of this belief. "He (God) is a rewarder of them that diligently seek him." (c) The Scriptural distinction between faith and sight is preserved. "We walk by faith not by sight" (II Cor. 5:7). (d) This definition recognizes faith's orientation toward the future. (e) A clear distinction is made between faith and belief. Faith and belief are not synonymous terms. Faith acts upon beliefs. (f) This definition accepts faith as a capability of the mind in the same sense that we believe in reason, judgment, love, etc. Faith involves the intellect, the will, and a conscious flavoring of emotion.

Faith is instrumental. It is not an end in itself, but a means to an end. It is a tool that is designed to give man an ability to deal with the future and the unseen. Through faith man can share in shaping and molding the future so as to attain his presently hoped for goals. These goals spring out of presently felt needs.

Several options (or beliefs) for meeting these needs may present themselves to the mind. They are out there in the future, maybe hours, months, or even years ahead of us. Reason will evaluate these options. One of them may appear to be the answer to the presently felt need. Belief emerges, and faith inspires a commitment and dedication to the pursuit and achievement of that goal. The line of movement is hearing, hope, reason, belief, faith, experience, and knowledge.

The distinction between faith and belief is made clear in this process. The chosen option must be a belief. This belief in turn becomes an object of faith. As an object of faith a belief becomes a principle by which we live. A belief, in and of itself, does not require commitment or action. But when a belief becomes an object of faith, then both commitment and action are required. Such beliefs guide and shape our actions (Peirce). Action must follow because the object of our faith lays upon us certain requirements. We are at the mercy of the objects of our faith. They dictate the requirements and the road we must follow to attain them. Thus, faith is living in the light and hope of a future experience. In this process, we can see how the future may influence the present.

Faith determines our present attitude, posture, and response to a hoped for goal or event that lies in the future. Faith concentrates and focuses our energies upon the "hoped for" goal of the future. This is illustrated by I John 3:2-3. Here the subject is the Second Coming of Christ. This is a belief. What should be our response to this belief as an object of faith? The Bible makes clear what our response should be, "And every man that hath this hope in him purifieth himself, even as he is pure." The Christian that hopes to meet the pure and holy Saviour is put under great pressure to be pure and holy himself. It is conceivable that an unsaved person may believe in the Second Coming of the Lord, but for him, it is only a belief and requires no action. He feels no compulsion to change his life style. The Second Coming is not a live option to him. It is not an object of faith for him.

Faith is creative. There are many things in the past and present that never would have come into existence if it had not been for someone's faith. William James said, "There are, then, cases where a fact cannot come at all unless a preliminary faith exists in its coming. And where faith in a fact can help create that fact" (*Will to Believe*). Thomas A. Edison believed that electricity could be used to produce light. His faith led him to conduct thousands of experiments before success crowned his efforts. All across the land we see church buildings, etc. that are a witness to faith. This creative aspect of faith is the greatest challenge that confronts us. This is a part of the divine image that man still possesses. Its potential for good or ill seems almost unlimited.

In Hebrews 11:1 there are at least two things said about faith. (1) Faith is the substance (or assurance) of things hoped for. A congregation hopes to build a new church on a certain site. It is faith that "assures" them that it can be done. It is faith that drives them to gather the "substance" necessary for constructing a new church. In due time that congregation will be worshipping God in a new sanctuary that faith "created."

(2) Faith is characterized as "evidence of things not seen." Now evidence is something that we use to prove that a thing is true or false. Things "hoped for" and "things not seen" are beyond the range of our physical senses. We cannot make physical contact with them. Thus we have to rely on some means of proof. Paul puts forth faith as "proof" at this point. Biblical faith has an emotional quality that produces in the heart a sense of assurance. This is interpreted by our minds as "proof." The impact of this "assurance" upon the mind and heart is something like that produced by self-evident truths. These truths need no lengthy demonstrations. For example, it does not take detailed arguments to prove that a whole is greater than any one of its parts. We can embrace such truths with the whole soul, mind, and

strength. Luther described this faith, "as a living daring confidence in God's grace. It is so sure that a man could stake his life on it a thousand times." (Bloesch).

On several occasions Jesus spoke of His disciples as "ye of little faith." After Pentecost the Bible speaks of them as being "full of faith." What made the difference? The baptism of the Holy Ghost! S. A. Keen says, "All lack of faith in true believers is the result of not having the baptism of the Holy Ghost" (*Faith Papers*). We struggle with little success to live a Christian life on what we should call, in most instances, the poverty level. Efforts are made to pump up (strengthen) our faith so we can enjoy a few spiritual luxuries. Success is not generous in crowning our efforts. "Faith cannot be trained into the stature of fullness. The fullness of faith is a produce of the baptism of the Holy Ghost" (Keen, *Faith Papers*). Biblical faith is a fruit of the Spirit (Gal. 5:22). The Christian life should be a full (abundant life: full of surrender, full of faith, full of wisdom, full of power, etc.) These come when we are full of the Holy Ghost.

CHAPTER 3

Why By Faith?

There are several reasons why God chose faith as the means to obtain salvation. (1) God is Spirit. This fact places God beyond the reach of those senses that are designed to operate in a material world. Concreteness very early becomes our measure of certainty and finality. We seek to live and move in a world of things that is easily verified by our senses. A world of solid, tangible things gives a certain comfort and assurance. But such a world makes up a relatively small part of our consciousness at any given moment.

Our "world" is like an iceberg; the major portion of it is hidden beneath the surface. The present moment of consciousness represents a small portion of this "world." The dimensions represented by the past and the future remain unseen. To these must be added the dimension of the spirit world. The past, the future, and the world of the spirit are the special domain of faith. Any part of our world which is not immediately present to the senses must be reached by faith. This applies with particular force to the things of the spirit.

Some persons seem to encourage the impression that faith is not necessary in the world of physical experience and that it is useful only in the unseen and uncertain world of religion. Nothing could be farther from the truth. Studies in epistemology reveal that we are of necessity shut-up into faith. Our reliance upon faith is as common to us as the material world. Those portions of the material world that are not immediately present to the senses must be reached by faith. Faith leads us to return to our parked car when we cannot see it. We have good reasons for believing it is still there and act accordingly. Such acts of faith are very common in everyday life. We are not strangers to the use of faith. That part of our world that is not now present to our senses can be acted upon as certainly as though it were present. This is exercising faith. In this sense faith is the bridge between the seen and the unseen; and the link that connects the present with the past and the future.

God is the great Unseen in our world. He never becomes concrete in the sense that a tree or mountain does while we are looking at them. We do not have to exercise faith to walk over and touch a tree we are looking at. But if that tree were hidden from view by, say a mountain, we would have to exercise faith if we touched it. The hope of touching it, plus good reasons for believing it is there, would spark faith which in turn would send us off to prove or disprove our hope. If the tree is there our faith is vindicated and it ends in the experience to which it led us. The movement of faith is from the unseen to the concrete or experienced.

All of this is very similar to our relationship with God. He comes to us at first as a hope. Reason assesses the probability of that hope. If it seems credible, then faith takes over and we respond in an appropriate manner. If the proper response is repentance at an altar of prayer and we follow through, we then experience God in the forgiveness of sins. This in a very real sense causes God to become "concrete" in our lives. He can never become concrete in the material sense that trees and mountains do but He does become a fact of experience. His lack of concreteness in a material sense makes it necessary that we conduct all of our business with Him by faith.

(2) Salvation is by faith because it is a universal possession of all human beings. Paul tells us in Romans 12:3 that God has given a measure of faith to all men. They not only possess it but they also use it in everyday life. The exercise of faith is one of the most common experiences known to man. A certain amount of faith is involved in about every decision we make and every act we perform.

Faith is an integral part of man and he cannot excuse his failure to be saved on the grounds that he did not have the means. The Bible says, "The word is nigh thee, even in thy mouth, and in thy heart: that is, the word of faith, which we preach" (Romans 10:8).

(3) Many times man must act upon that which is not presently within the circle of his consciousness, and many times he must act upon something that is dimly understood. These gaps are bridged by faith. In these cases faith precedes

—15—

knowledge by actual experience. Such ventures of faith do not argue that faith sometimes has nothing back of it but a sheer act of the will. Such a situation, it would seem, could occur only in the realm of the theoretical. In actual experience the act of faith certainly rests upon what is accepted as sufficient evidence. Acting upon anything less is to skate upon the thin ice of superstition.

(4) Faith bridges the gaps between the past, present, and the future. A childish mind is completely involved with the existential Now, the present. But a mature mind cannot sever its ties with the past nor can it ignore the future. Faith must deal with these "intangibles." The past cannot be changed but the future can be. It does not have to duplicate the past. We can quarry from the past and build a future to our liking. We invest in the Now and clip the coupons in the future. This is acting on faith.

(5) Again God chose faith as the means of salvation to exclude the possibility of man's boasting (Romans 3:27). Jesus called attention to this sin in the parable of the Pharisee and publican at prayer (Luke 18:9-14). Salvation by faith nips this sin in the bud.

(6) Salvation must be by faith because it is by grace (Ephesians 2:8). God did not act arbitrarily but He was guided by the facts of man's predicament. Man's situation under the perfect law of God was hopeless. He had broken the perfect law and divine justice demanded punishment. There was (and is) nothing that man could do to extricate himself from his predicament. No expressions of sorrow or ever so many promises not to do it again would avail. There were no sacrifices of labor or self-denials that could atone for his sin. There were no legal grounds upon which God could act. God's act of salvation had to be a special act based upon His absolute sovereignty. It was motivated by love; its justification was mercy, and its application was grace. There was no place for works (Romans 4:1-5).

However, men still strongly insist upon salvation by works. A little reflection will reveal several bad features of such a system. (a) It could exclude God, and (b) it certainly would exclude some men. No system of works could be devised that would be within the capabilities of all men. Then (c) there would be the problem of the kinds of works to be performed. Along with this it (d) would be necessary to determine the quantity and quality of these works. The end result of such a system would be that every man would do that which was right in his own sight.

(7) Our last consideration will be the impact of faith upon the individual. In the first place, faith not only accepts the existence of God but also makes Him the most important object of our lives. Faith locks us onto God and His will becomes the guiding force that gives direction to all of life. In other words, faith will prevent the scattering of our energies and will bring them to focus upon God. Secondly, faith inspires obedience. God puts a high premium upon obedience. In His estimation, "To obey is better than sacrifice, and to hearken than the fat of rams" (I Samuel 15:22). God delights in the return of the prodigal son and He gladly extends mercy and grace but He is surely much more pleased if disobedience does not occur.

Thirdly, faith strongly influences our love for God. In the beginning our relationship to God is determined more by a sense of fear or duty. Under the benevolent influence of faith this grows into a deep, abiding love. Closely related to this is the fourth influence of faith. It sensitizes the conscience. God becomes so real and precious to the faithful that any failure results in a broken heart and a contrite spirit. This is of special importance because God seeks such to save (Psalm 34:18) and it marks the dividing line between the genuine child of God and the pretender.

This is the difference between King Saul and King David. both sinned against God and both confessed. Saul, with an often repeated "I have sinned"; but David, with the fifty-first Psalm. King Saul failed to find acceptance with God but David was forgiven and often acclaimed to be a man after God's own heart.

The fifth and final impact of faith upon the believer that we wish to consider is that faith motivates to action. It cannot remain as mere mental assent nor as a spectator, it must become involved in good works whereunto we have been created (Ephesians 2:10). Faith that fails to be fruitful is described by the apostle James as being dead (2:20-26). Faith must be fruitful if it is to survive.

God chose faith as the means to salvation because there was no other suitable way. It meets man's need; it is available to all and it satisfies the righteousness of God.

CHAPTER 4

The Bible and Faith

Jesus on several occasions spoke of faith. His life is the supreme example of living by faith. He practiced what He preached. The result was that His story is the "greatest story ever told" of the "greatest life ever lived." Faith gave direction and consistency to His life. From the manger-cradle to the cross there were no detours. Faith held Him to His mission. Faith gave Him a sense of power, not only for the routine of life, but also for the special occasions. Every miracle was the result of faith. His intimacy and ready access to God rested upon His unwavering faith. He could lift his eyes heavenward and pray, "Father, I thank thee that thou hast heard me. And I know that thou hearest me always" (John 11:41-42). This faith He sought to instill in the hearts of His disciples. On many occasions He pointed out to them that their failure was the direct result of weak faith. Many times He challenged them with the great potential of faith, "whatsoever ye shall ask" (John 14:13).

Jesus was concerned not only about the faith of His disciples but also about the faith of those that should believe down through the centuries until He returned in power and glory. It would seem that He was not so optimistic because He said on one occasion, "Nevertheless when the Son of man cometh, shall he find faith on the earth?" (Luke 18:8). The question seems to anticipate a negative answer. Paul speaks of religion in the last days as having a form of godliness but denying the power thereof" (2 Timothy 3:5). Here we see faith so perverted that it is unable to grasp anything more than the shell of religion. Beyond the shell we meet with rank unbelief, "denying the power thereof." Here is the sad picture of a professed faith that no longer leads to a life filled and energized by the Holy Spirit, but to the whitewashed tombs in the graveyard of unbelief. Under such circumstances it is not going to be easy to find and exercise genuine Biblical faith. We can avoid being trapped only by carefully examining ourselves to see if we are "in the faith." For further light on faith let us turn to the great apostle to the Gentiles and attempt to discover how he understood and practiced faith. It can be safely said that none of the New Testament writers had a better understanding of the nature of faith and of its place in God's plan of redemption than the apostle Paul.

According to him, faith was a common possession of all men (Romans 12:3). It is by faith that we please God because we believe "that he is and that he is a rewarder of them that diligently seek him" (Heb. 11:6). "Faith is the substance of things hoped for, the evidence of things not seen" (Heb. 11:1). Faith is the shield of faith that protects from the fiery darts that radiate from the enemy (Eph. 6:16). It is by faith that the promises of God are received and in turn it is this faith that God accepts as a substitute for righteousness (Rom. 4:9, 23-25). Such a faith is no mean thing; it is a challenge both to the learned and the unlearned.

Paul's theology of salvation had two major themes. The first was "that Christ died for our sins according to the scriptures; and that he was buried, and that he rose again the third day according to the scriptures" (I Cor. 15:3-4). His second theme was that faith is the means by which this atonement is received and becomes a personal reality (Rom. 3:21-26). This is a long ways from what Paul had been taught as a young man and what he had practiced before he met Christ.

His former religious life had been built upon a foundation of works. This was basically the faithful keeping of the law. His nation was committed to this idea and it was also basic in the religious practices of the pagan world. From Paul's own testimony we learn that he had given himself wholeheartedly to the practice of his religion (Gal. 1:14; Phil. 3:4-6). But we also learn that his achievements in the religion of his people did not satisfy his heart. In the seventh chapter of Romans, we have an analysis of his experience under the law. His blamelessness as touching the law did not satisfy the yearning for pure motives and a pure heart. Covetousness stirred in his heart; his great accomplishments in his religious pursuit made him a proud man. His successes were dogged by defeat (Romans 7:1-25). Then he met Jesus.

The meeting came at the height of his campaign in the defense of the faith of his fathers. It came as he was about to strike another solid blow against the "fanatics" among the faithful. The caliber of the man can be judged by the means God used to stop him. And it can also be judged by his response to the revelation of Jesus Christ. He was a man of perception and understanding. There was no haggling, nor sense of loss, even though his "blameless" religious record lay with him in the dust of the Damascus road. He rejoiced to leave it there. His good works were no longer jewels in his crown of self-righteousness. No longer was he fascinated and drawn by their sparkle and glitter; rather he turned from them as from a repulsive and foul smelling manure pile (Phil. 3:4-8). This was about as radical a change as can be experienced by any human being. Such a change must be accompanied by a new theology.

Paul's new doctrine of atonement stands as a stark contrast to his old system, even though the new had been present in the old. It is a classic example of the transformation that can be wrought by a change in perspective. The Jews had failed to place the elements of God's redemptive plan together correctly and they had emphasized the wrong things. It took a miracle of grace and divine revelation to untangle and straighten out Paul's theology. Thank God, he was willing to change his mind! God's plan of redemption in all of its majestic power and simplicity took shape in his mind. Every part—faith, law, the prophets, and Calvary— fell into place. He saw that from the very beginning God had chosen to justify the sinner by faith. The giving of the law had not superseded this plan. With great skill Paul developed this thesis in his polemics with the Jews.

To support his contention he reached back into the history of Israel for an example of a man that had been justified by faith. This man was the patriarch, Abraham. Paul was on safe ground here because no Jew would question the experience of Abraham, the venerable founder of their nation. The specific experience of Abraham cited by Paul is recorded in Genesis 15:6. He also builds on two other passages of Scripture. David in Psalm 32:1 is interpreted by Paul as teaching justification by faith (Romans 4:6-8). Again, Paul quotes Habakkuk 2:4 as a proof-text for his position (Romans 1:17). Thus Paul is thoroughly Biblical in his approach.

The particular experience of Abraham to which Paul calls attention is not the first time that Abraham believed God. He had been walking by faith a good many years. When God called him in Ur of the Chaldees to leave his own country, he packed up and left by faith, not knowing where he was going. He stopped at Haran but again the call came and he continued his journey by faith. His life in the Promised Land was one of faith because the land was still possessed by the Canaanites and they had no intention of vacating for him. So "possession" had to be by faith. To test his faith even further, God had not given Abraham a son. What good would the Promised Land be if he left no posterity to fill it?

As the years passed, no doubt Abraham became more concerned about the lack of an heir. This was a faith situation of the first magnitude, but Abraham was equal to the situation, and came through with flying colors. God was not unmindful of Abraham's need and concern. It is well to note here that faith always relates to needs. They may be personal or they may relate to God's people or to the glory of God. In any case, faith is always related to a genuine need. It is not subject to whims or fancied needs. Faith reaches out to an object that can meet a need. Here Abraham's great need was a son. God addressed Himself to that need and gave Abraham, not a son, but a promise of one. The promise came too late! He and Sarah were long past the age when they could hope to have children. This was compounding the test of Abraham's faith, but Paul says, "He staggered not" (Rom. 4:20). There had been no time limit set for the fulfillment of the promise. Many years rolled by before the promise was fulfilled. What a time of testing it must have been! But Abraham was "fully persuaded" (Rom. 4:21). In God's good time the son arrived. Abraham's need was met and the lineage of the promised "Seed" was assured.

Abraham's faith was twice blessed. He not only received his heir, which was in itself a sufficient reward, but God added an even greater blessing. He reckoned his faith unto him as righteousness (Gen. 15:6). In other words, God accepted Abraham's faith as a substitute for righteousness. The apostle Paul bases his doctrine of justification by faith upon this simple and almost obscure transaction in the life of Abraham (Rom. 4:23-24).

This concept, like another of Paul's concepts, is subject to perversion. It appears that some misunderstood or wrested his statement, "But where sin abounded, grace did much more abound" (Rom. 5:20) into meaning that we must continue abounding in sin in order to enjoy continued abounding grace. This interpretation of Paul was "made to order" for the lover of sin, but it did violence to the intent of the apostle. His reaction was a quick and emphatic "God forbid" (Rom. 6:2). The experience of God's grace is not limited to the forgiveness of sins. It is a "manifold grace" (1 Peter 4:10). Its acceptance renders the continuance in sin impossible (Rom. 6:1-7).

Any perversion of the concept that faith is a substitute for righteousness arises out of a mistaken idea of faith. This danger does not exist in the case of true Biblical faith. But some may immediately jump to the conclusion that anything we call faith will substitute for righteousness. This is far from the truth; God does not cast His pearls before swine. All men have faith (Rom. 12:3), but it does not follow that all men will be justified. This would be universalism with a bang. Salvation does not hinge upon the possession of faith but upon the use of it. Abraham was rewarded not because he possessed faith, but for correctly using his faith. He believed God. His exercise of faith made it consistent for God to exercise grace in his behalf. In the final analysis, faith is not the most important factor in a faith situation. The most important factor is the object of faith.

God's control of the objects of faith permits Him to throw open the doors of His storehouse to the faithful. There is no danger of selfish plundering of His riches or the misuse of faith. God's promises, as the objects of faith, are designed to accomplish His will in the heart and life of the believer. Thus, if the repentant sinner pleads the blood of Christ and believes God's promises of forgiveness, his faith will be rewarded by receiving forgiveness and reconciliation. He will experience the new birth and become a new creature in Christ Jesus. When the obedient child of God makes the promise of the Holy Spirit the object of faith he will receive the baptism of the Holy Spirit. Biblical faith can never be exercised for idle display. It must always be used to meet individual needs, or the need of the Church, or to glorify God, etc.

God has predestined all who choose to live in this manner to enjoy eternity with Him. All who choose not to live the Christ-like life are predestined to live in eternity without God and without hope. Predestination is a matter of class action, and not an individual matter. The individual is responsible for choosing the group he desires to be identified with but God determines the ultimate destiny of the groups, saints or sinners.

CHAPTER 5

Faith and Its Objects

Faith is not something that occupies at all times a central place in our consciousness. Most of the time we are unaware that we are exercising faith. However, it is present in most situations in life. Theoretically we may conceive of pure "faith" situations or pure "sight" situations, but in real life it is doubtful if they exist. Faith, like love, takes on an emotional aspect and rises to the conscious level whenever it is engaged with an object in a particular way.

Faith as a capacity or ability is not "born" when confronted by an object. The ability to exercise faith is always present. It is proper, however, to say that faith in a certain object is "born" at a given point in time. In some instances it may be faith at first "sight." In others, a long intellectual struggle may take place before faith is "born."

An object of faith may be anything that is not immediately present to the senses. Anything that has become a matter of experience cannot be an object of faith. Experience transforms faith objects into what we think of as proven concrete facts. They take on a different character and play a different role in our lives. Faith reaches out ahead of actual experience to that which we hope will someday become actual experience. These objects may be just about anything that the mind can conceive. They may be an idea, a concept, a proposition, or some material object.

The Bible throws some light on how something may become an object of faith. In Romans 10:13-15 these steps are presented. The hope of salvation is the subject under discussion. Paul is in the process of showing that the old system of law was unable to provide the desired salvation. In its place he presents the Gospel of the Lord Jesus Christ. Hearing the Gospel kindles a hope that perhaps this is the way to salvation. Reason assesses the merits of this hope on the basis of the evidence that is available. If reason unites with hope in a favorable judgment, faith in the Lord Jesus is born.

A critical phase in this development must be examined a little more closely. Reason may accept the fact that Jesus Christ is the Saviour of all that call upon Him in faith and yet fail to take the step of commitment. Belief is not the same as faith. A part of our freedom lies in the fact that we do not have to commit ourselves to our beliefs. For one reason or another we can choose to permit them to become nothing more than mere beliefs. We choose the beliefs that we wish to elevate to the level of principles that we live by and will conform to our desired pattern of life. In this way we become architects of our personality and character. We choose to commit ourselves to certain objects or beliefs because they represent what we really wish to receive or become.

Some think that faith is passive and does nothing but receive the desired object. In some instances this may be true, but in most instances faith acts as a powerful motivating drive. Faith is not a lazy man's tool. Men of faith are men of action. They do not sit and wait for God to act. Their faith is locked on an object out there in the future. It does not come to them, they must go to it. By the help of God, their determination is to reach it.

The objects of faith dictate the road we must travel to reach them. This fact is true in science as well as in religious matters. We do not take it upon ourselves to decide what steps we wish to take to reach the object of our faith. The necessary steps are pre-determined and it is our task to discover them. Edison believed that he could produce an incandescent light. He did not try to dictate to nature how this was to be accomplished. His faith drove him to perform thousands of experiments to discover the natural conditions that would make an incandescent light possible. Faith operates in religious matters exactly as it does in science.

Objects of faith in the religious realm are just as dictatorial as they are in the fields of science. We do not lay down the rules, they do. It is our duty to obey the rules and to seek out the path that will lead us to the object of our faith. To put it another way, we can say that the response to an object of faith is pre-determined. We are not compelled to make the response but if we desire to reach that particular objective the pre-determined response is the only one that will be successful. One reason for God's choosing faith as a substitute for righteousness lies in the fact that He determines the objects of our faith. Our pursuit of these objectives leads us to live in the same manner we would live if we were truly righteous.

It must be kept in mind that faith is oriented to the future. Faith looks forward to that which is yet to come. Walking by faith is to "see" the objective out there in the future and to direct our lives in a manner that will lead to that goal. Faith's overall purpose is to lead to actual experience.

The objects of faith do not change; we must adjust our lives to meet their demands. This is what the Bible means when it says, "But we all, with open face beholding as in a glass the glory of the Lord, are changed into the same image from glory to glory, even as by the Spirit of the Lord" (II Cor. 3:18). An object of faith in the distant future may be dimly seen and poorly understood. As we draw nearer to it, we come to better understand its demands upon us and we make the necessary adjustments. Faith makes it possible for us to shape, at least in part, our future world.

Not all beliefs are of equal importance. We actually use very few of them in shaping our selves and our world. I believe that there was a Roman emperor named Tiberius Caesar. This belief does not have to be seriously considered as I plan my life. Tiberius had, in a distant province, a humble subject called Jesus of Nazareth. I cannot ignore Him as I do Caesar. He and Caesar are historical figures, but I have reasons to believe that the Nazarene is more important to me than Caesar. I make Christ the supreme object of my faith. Caesar remains a mere historical figure.

By faith we adopt certain beliefs that we consider most important to us. These become the principles by which we live. They shape and mold us and determine our character. Charles Peirce, an American philosopher, points out that such beliefs take on the nature of habits. They control our responses so that we tend to respond to certain situations in the same way each time we are confronted with that particular situation.

Faith objects are legion in number and they vary in significance from the meaningless to the most important things that can engage the minds of men. At first we may be like children in a toy shop dashing from one toy to another. Sooner or later we must make choices and a pattern begins to emerge. We must adopt a world view. These come in two styles: one has God in it and the other one does not. No greater choice than this can confront an individual. There is a vast difference between a world with God in it and a world without God. By faith (it can be no other way) we must adopt one or the other of these world views. We cannot be neutral nor can we have both.

It would appear that if we adopt a world view with God in it, that He would automatically become the Supreme Object of our faith. This is not the way it works out. God remains just one of our beliefs unless we choose to do something about it. He cannot become the Supreme Object of our faith unless we give Him that position. If this is not done, it does not follow that that person is an atheist but it does mean that God is ranked on the same level as all other beliefs. It will be an important one to be sure but still just a belief. A person in this situation would be what might be called a practical atheist. They live as though God does not exist. Their mistake is that they have not taken the step of faith and committed themselves to God as the Supreme Object of their faith. He does not become the Principle to live by; He does not become a "habit."

There are two things that need to be emphasized at this point. (1) The critical point in the faith-object relationship is whether or not there is a commitment to the object of faith. This is extremely important. The strength or weakness of faith emerges at this point. Every effort should be made to prepare and condition the sinner to realize that this commitment must be unconditional and a total surrender to the object of their faith, the Lord Jesus Christ. This is not to be confused with the process of being convinced that a thing is true and thus it becomes one of our beliefs. We are confronted here with the next step beyond belief. A belief may or may not be important to us. If there seems to be something vital and important in a belief we are likely to give it some thought and consideration. After reflecting upon the matter, a judgment is rendered. It may be a positive or negative judgment. If it is seen that belief in Christ will bring to one's life many desirable things, a decision is made to make that belief the keystone of one's life. This step must be taken by faith. Faith requires a total commitment to all that Christ represents or stands for in this life and the hereafter.

(2) The next important thing to notice is that many faith-objects have no power within themselves to help the believer. Thomas A. Edison committed himself to the idea of an incandescent light, but that idea had no power to help him to achieve his goal. This is not true when God is the object of faith. He actively enters into the situation and assists the faithful to achieve the object of their faith. This is particularly true when faith is exercised to enter God's redemptive plan.

The Old Testament experience shows that man needs more than forgiveness and reconciliation to God to have victory over sin. God, through the prophets, promised that some day He would pour out His Spirit upon all flesh (Ezekiel 36:24-27; Joel 2:28). Jesus commanded the disciples to tarry in Jerusalem until God fulfilled this promise (Acts 1:4-5, 8). Peter calls attention to this same promise (Acts 2:38-39).

Without going into too many details, let us trace the steps necessary to receive the gift of the Holy Spirit. The Gospel must be presented in a manner that will condition sinners so that their expectation will be to follow the example of the Lord Jesus in His Jordan River experiences. We must emphasize that to receive the forgiveness of our sins, several things are required. (a) There must be a genuine godly sorrow and confession of the sins committed. (b) This must be accompanied by true repentance in turning from the sinful life. (c) Repentance must include a total unconditional surrender to God. (d) On the positive side, the sinner must make a total commitment to the Lord Jesus and all that He represents. It is difficult to believe that God will or can declare a sinner justified on anything less than this.

When the repenting sinner receives the witness of God's forgiveness, he is immediately a candidate to receive the gift of the Holy Spirit. The house has been swept and garnished and made ready for the new occupant (Matt. 12:43-45). A new convert should be encouraged to seek immediately the gift of the Holy Spirit. He will never have a better opportunity to receive the Spirit than immediately after conversion. This is not only the most favorable time but it is also the time of greatest need. The new babe in Christ is not very well equipped to face a hostile world. It is the hour of deepest need. The presence of the indwelling Comforter is crucial. The new babe in Christ cannot survive without the strengthening might of the Holy Spirit.

There can be no question about God's willingness to give the Holy Spirit to them that ask for the heavenly Guest. Jesus assures us that our heavenly Father is more willing to give the Holy Spirit to those that ask for Him than parents are to give good gifts to their children (Luke 11:13). The joyous experience of being forgiven and reconciled with God should not be allowed to obscure the need of immediately asking the Father for the gift of the Holy Spirit. Failure to do this leads to disaster. The evil spirit, with his pals, will move back into the empty house and the situation will be worse than it was before he had been cast out. Charles G. Finney said that his observations led him to believe that if the new converts did not immediately seek and receive the Holy Spirit, they inevitably would backslide.

Those of the Wesleyan persuasion have been making a terrible mistake at this point. We have accepted the long delay as "normal." This, I am convinced, has resulted in a great deal of confusion and the ultimate loss of countless numbers of souls. Holiness preachers advise new converts to go out and live for the Lord and some day they will discover that they have a carnal heart. When they discover this and God convicts them of the need of a clean heart, they should then seek a clean heart or entire sanctification. This is too late! Carnal manifestations indicate that the evil spirit and his pals have moved back into the swept and garnished house. We are now faced with something more than remaining carnality. It would seem that souls in this condition would have to do the first step over again and then move on to the second step, the filling of the Holy Spirit. No doubt some who are seeking holiness should be seeking restoration from a backslidden condition. In the process they may experience renewal and they mistake it for the baptism of the Holy Spirit. The result is they become very poor examples of the Spirit filled life.

No new convert should leave the altar of prayer without being instructed to immediately ask the Father for the gift of the Holy Spirit. A time of prayer should follow, seeking the outpouring of the Spirit upon the new convert. The preaching of the Gospel should have prepared them to follow the example of the Lord Jesus in His Jordan River experiences. It might be well to revive the practice of laying on of hands.

CHAPTER 6

Faith as a Substitute for Righteousness

The importance of faith can be seen in the fact that God accepts it as a substitute for righteousness. This fact staggers our minds. Yet no truth is more solidly grounded in the Scripture than this one. We are justified by faith and we are filled with the Holy Spirit by faith. The Christian life from its beginning to the end is a walk by faith.

God can accept faith as a substitute for righteousness because it motivates men to live like a righteous man would live. Many men and women of the Bible illustrate this fact. The eleventh chapter of Hebrews lists a few of these. It is true, they were not perfect but we must not forget that they were not living under the level of salvation provided in Christ nor did they enjoy the revelation of God that we have in Christ. Their faith motivated them to live up to the level of the revelation that they had. This is why God accepted them and reckoned their faith as righteousness.

Our Lord is the only man that ever lived a truly faithful and righteous life. He was holy in stature and perfectly expressed this in a life of righteousness. His supreme concern was to do the will of Him that had sent Him into this world. This perfect man and this perfect life is forever our ideal and our example.

Redeemed man cannot rise to this level of righteousness in this life. With the help of God's grace our best can only be relative to that ideal. By faith we look for that perfect redemption which shall be ours when Christ comes in His glory and we shall see Him as He is (I John 3:1-3). Until that great day our faith keeps us in step with God's provision for us in the here and now. The Bible says, "And every man that hath this hope in him purifieth himself, even as he is pure" (verse 3).

A word needs to be said about the expression of relativism in the above paragraph. One hesitates to use the term because of its current misuse. Some are using it to describe a system of philosophy that denies the existence of absolute standards in ethics and values. This is the philosophy back of the insistence that everyone has a right to do his own "thing." Everyone determines for himself what he thinks is right. No greater license to commit evil of every sort has ever been granted than that provided by this philosophy. In the final analysis it knows no self-restraint or discipline other than that which men may choose to impose. God's law does not exist for them. We have to learn by trial and error whether a thing is good or bad.

We cannot deny that relativism exists. It does, and this world is a veritable "thicket" of relativism. True relativism exists between the ideal and the concrete situation. The ideal is the absolute standard and the application of that standard to the concrete situation can be nothing other than relative. It is a fact of life that our application of the perfect will of God to real life situations is always something less than perfect. Some take advantage of this and accept it as a license to live careless and even sinful lives. True faith, the faith that substitutes for righteousness, will not permit this to happen. The fact that our application of God's standard is relative does not in any fashion minimize the grace of God. His grace lifts us to that level of salvation He has provided for this life. Perfect redemption must wait until we are glorified with Christ.

The pattern of life that Biblical faith establishes and the pattern established by holiness of nature is much alike. As noted before, the Lord Jesus Christ is forever our example. This is the ideal that God has set before us (Romans 8:29). True Biblical faith will powerfully motivate men to conform to this ideal. Our success will be largely determined by how earnestly and diligently we give ourselves to this quest.

Many careless, lukewarm, professing Christians fail at this point. They make only a feeble effort to approximate that ideal example which our Lord has left us. They fail for several reasons. First, they fail because they do not heed the commandment to put on the whole armor of God (Ephesians 6:13). They may readily enough seek God for forgiveness and reconciliation, but then they make their big mistake by failing to seek that strengthening with might by His Spirit in the inner man (Ephesians 3:16). This strengthening can come only by the baptism and filling of the Holy Ghost. This deficiency is extremely dangerous and can be fatal. It accounts for the poor state of the average Christian's professed witness for Christ.

The first failure leads to the second failure. The many defeats of the Christian that does not have this inner strengthening by the Holy Spirit will lead to an overwhelming sense of the power of sin and the weakness of human nature. They come to identify their sins as nothing more than mere expressions of the weakness of human nature. Their aim is to keep these at a minimum. In the third place, the lack of the Holy Spirit in His teaching ministry results in an inability to distinguish between downright sin and true human frailties. The result of this is that they make no sustained effort to conform to the image of God's Son. Biblical faith will not permit us to be satisfied with such a shabby witness to God's power to save.

We will have to pause and note that no level of salvation in this life frees us from problems, frailties, and human limitations. God bestows upon us a great salvation in reconciliation and the gift of the Holy Spirit. The application of this great experience to everyday life is not always easy. There are frailties that have been intensified by sin. Our thinking and judgment have been impaired by sin. Human limitations constantly confront us. The flesh tires and grows weak and we see through a glass darkly. It must always be kept in mind that "we have this treasure in earthen vessels" (II Corinthians 4:7). We must always work out our own salvation with fear and trembling (Philippians 2:12).

These weaknesses and failures should in no way become excuses for clearly obvious acts of sin. The apostle had in mind true weaknesses of the human situation. This involves such things as a lack of perfect judgment that leads to errors and mistakes, slowness to learn and to act properly. There may be misinterpretations of others' motives. Many other things could be listed. In no case should obvious non-Christian actions and attitudes be accepted. Human weakness does not cover lying, profanity, cheating, immorality, hatred, etc.

All of this points up the fact that human nature, though cleansed by the blood of Christ, still bears the scars and crippling effects of sin. This makes it impossible for redeemed man to possess in this life that perfect holiness which we see in the Lord Jesus. The enjoyment of that holiness will have to await glorification in the world to come. Until then God is willing to accept our faith as a substitute for that righteousness which we do not now possess (Romans 4:1-8, 20-25).

God can accept this substitution for several reasons. Firstly, Biblical faith accepts the existence of God and conforms life to a pattern that is in harmony with that belief. This will be the perfect intention of the heart but the finished product may not be so perfect. The frailties, etc., mentioned above, may lead to some rough spots. However, God will not hold these things against His children. He will accept their faith as righteousness and He will not "impute sin" to them.

Secondly, God can accept faith as a substitute for righteousness because faith expects God to reward those that diligently seek Him (Hebrews 11:6). This opens the way for God to do many wonderful things for those that believe. Read once again the eleventh chapter of Hebrews and pay particular attention to the things that God did in response to their faith. Add to these the many wonderful promises that God has given to us in the Gospel. Surely, God has withheld no good thing from them that walk uprightly (Psalm 84:11).

Thirdly, the posture of faith is the same as that of righteousness. It orients man toward God. As the guidance mechanism of a space ship locks on a certain star to hold the ship on its course, so faith locks the soul on God and holds it steadily on its course. Isaiah describes this as a mind that is stayed on God (26:3). Thus, faith keeps man moving in the right direction.

Fourthly, faith is open-endedness toward God. The lines of communication are open. It is also an expression of receptivity. This is a "hot" line directly from the soul to God. There are no dials, centrals, or other parties on the line to slow things up. Communication is directly and instantly established. God communicates with man not only by the prayer line but also through His Word. The Word of God is the final test of all things, even that which comes over the prayer line. It is the source of the promises that become the objects of faith. Through these promises our needs are met. The Bible should be a very familiar book to the child of God.

In the fifth place, faith produces the same attitude towards God that righteousness would produce. Faith is an expression of man's inmost being. It thus expresses man's real attitude towards God. Biblical faith motivates man to seek and maintain normal relations with God. He will come to God in genuine repentance and see for reconciliation with God. After his acceptance by God he will seek the fulfillment of God's promise to give him the Holy Spirit to abide in his heart and to empower him for victorious living and witnessing. Nothing greater than this can happen to anyone in this life. Through faith a vile body is transformed into the dwelling place of God. This is indeed the fulfillment of the prophecy of Ezekiel 36:24-28.

Faith assures an attitude of obedience. The will of God becomes the deepest concern of one who has attained this wonderful relationship with God. Every effort will be made to assure obedience. The Psalmist illustrates this when he says, "Set a watch, O Lord, before my mouth" (141:3). Here the Psalmist was praying for victory over the second most vulnerable area of his life, his speech. He was aware of the danger of sinning against God in his speech. In another place he says, "My heart is fixed on God." He knew the safety that lies in having some things settled for all time. Another precaution that he took to assure obedience was to hide God's word in his heart (Psalm 119:11).

Faith also insures a genuine repentance if failure does occur. Forgiveness is sought with a broken heart and a contrite spirit. The fifty-first Psalm is the finest expression of this spirit to be found anywhere in the literature of the human family. David not only made his confession verbally, he sat down and wrote it out in black and white.

Finally, the sixth reason why faith is a substitute for righteousness is because it corrects man's perspective. Without Biblical faith man turns inward and sees himself as the most important thing in the universe. This distortion leads to all kinds of problems, both personal and social. Inner conflicts arise because man was created for greater things than the worship of himself. His relations to others cannot be normal and sometimes they become vicious. Faith properly relates man to God, the universe, society, and to himself.

CHAPTER 7

Jesus, Our Example

Basically, the Lord Jesus came to do three things. (1) He came to provide Redemption for those of Adam's descendants that might wish to escape the power and penalty of sin. (2) He came to reveal the steps necessary to participate in the plan of Redemption. (3) His brief ministry showed how the redeemed life is to be lived. We will consider each of the points in the above order.

We cannot comprehend what it cost God to be just and the justifier of those that believe in Jesus. God cannot arbitrarily brush aside sin. Sin is rebellion against the will and authority of God. No authority can lightly accept such a challenge.

The awful price that the human family has paid for sin is beyond our comprehension. Experts estimate that the number of persons slain in all past wars is equal to the 1983 population of the world. Who can comprehend the suffering and agony involved in all of that dying? But this is not the whole story. We must add to this all the suffering and agony caused by sin in the day by day activities of sinful people. We cannot comprehend the hurt caused by the lying, thefts, murders, deceit, gossip, etc., and the end is not in sight. Eternity presents a fearsome picture.

Who knows what sin will cost the sinner out there in eternity without God? The Bible presents this in very grim terms. It speaks of a place of eternal torment where the "worm dieth not and the fire is not quenched" (Isaiah 66:24). "The smoke of their torment ascendeth up for ever and ever" (Rev. 14:11). Jesus told about a rich man that missed heaven and found himself in hell (Luke 16:19-31). The practice of sin is not free—the cost is staggering, in the present life and in the life out there in eternity. God cannot simply brush sin aside and say, "Let's forget it." He did, however, provide a way to escape the power and penalty of sin.

The cost of Redemption was high. God could not choose a cheap way out of man's predicament. His justice and righteousness were at stake. He had to provide a plan that all intelligent beings, angels, devils, and men would have to acknowledge as just and fair. God had to tap the resources of the Trinity to provide the cost of Redemption. Divine justice had to be satisfied and the raging of evil powers had to be stopped. The Son of God was appointed to undertake the mission of Redemption.

This mission of Redemption was undertaken for the fallen race of Adam. It did not include fallen angels. It should also be noted that Paul suggests that there is such a thing as a lack in the sufferings of Christ for the Church, the body of Christ. Paul rejoiced that he had the opportunity to help fill that need (Col. 1:24). The great apostle rejoiced that he was privileged to share in the redemptive sufferings of Christ for the Church.

In the human family, Jesus was the Son of God. He was not sired by a man, but became a member of the human family by the virgin birth. He was in a unique sense the Son of Man. His relationship to the Divine and the human race was very real. In Him, a "new Creation" came into existence, born of God and born of Adam's race. He is the Son of God and the Son of Man.

The incarnation was necessary for several reasons. (a) It placed the Lord Jesus in position to become our Kinsman Redeemer. This is beautifully presented in the Bible in the book of Ruth. As a result of a drought and famine, Elimelech, Naomi, and their two sons, left Bethlehem in Judah and went down to Moab, a traditional enemy of the Israelites. They had heard that there was food in Moab. There greater misfortunes befell them. The husband, Elimelech, died. Naomi's two sons married Moabite women. Soon both of the sons died. At this juncture, Naomi heard that the drought in Judah had ended. Naomi and Ruth returned to Bethlehem. Naomi faced the problem of recovering her husband's property. A near relative, Boaz by name, acting as kinsman redeemer, recovered the property and took Ruth to be his wife. Ruth, the Moabite, became the mother of a son. This son became an ancestor of King David, who in turn became an ancestor of the Lord Jesus Christ.

(b) As a member of the human family, the Lord Jesus was tempted in all points as any other human being. But unlike human beings, He did not fall into sin. He demonstrated that a human body does not necessitate sinning.

(c) His experience in the flesh enabled Him to become a sympathetic and understanding High Priest.

(d) In the flesh He set before us the pattern of life that His followers should pursue.

The greatest life ever lived provoked a varied response. Many enthusiastically accepted Him. Others, stung by His verbal barbs, bitterly hated Him. This hatred ultimately nailed Him to the cross. It is difficult to understand the spirit of that hatred of the Lord. They were willing to cut short the life of one that had delivered many from their bodily afflictions. The lame walked and leaped for joy. The blind were made to see. Even the dead arose and walked away from the bier and the grave. If He could have lived many more years, He would have healed many more of the afflicted. Those that were denied healing by the crucifixion will surely rise up at the judgment and condemn the rulers for their insensibility to their sufferings.

The victory of the forces of evil was short. They were soon confronted with a new problem. The rulers had anticipated this problem and had tried to guard against it. They made the tomb as secure as they could. It certainly was an exercise in futility. The eternal almighty Son of God could not be sealed in a grave, though hewn out of the rock. On that first Easter morning, a powerful angel rolled the stone away from the entrance of the tomb. It was not to permit the resurrected Lord to come out of the tomb, but to permit His followers to enter the tomb. The Roman guards had fled into the city. It must have been a frustrating time for the enemies of the Lord. They did the best they could with a bad situation by spreading false rumors.

On the other side of the struggle, the disciples were trying to put things together. The empty tomb and the several appearances of the Lord certainly lifted their spirits. They were beginning to share in the victory of their Lord. It was their privilege to meet with the Lord on several occasions over the next forty days. In His last appearance (Acts 1:1-11) He commanded them to tarry in Jerusalem until they be endued with power from on high (Luke 24:29). After His ascension they did return to Jerusalem and "were continually in the temple, praising and blessing God" (Luke 24:52-53).

After ten days of "tarrying" the great day came. "They were all with one accord and in one place. And suddenly there came a sound from heaven as of a rushing mighty wind, and filled all the house where they were sitting. And there appeared unto them cloven tongues like as of fire, and sat upon each of them. And they were all filled with the Holy Ghost" (Acts 2:1-4). The hour was nine o'clock in the morning (Acts 2:15). Their days of tarrying were over. They rushed out of the building where they had been sitting, filled with a dynamic power that transformed them.They were no longer on the defensive, keeping a low profile. They launched a major offensive.

Peter's sermon to the multitude that was attracted by the events that had just transpired could be considered rash and unwise. It would certainly seem risky to condemn the multitude for having crucified the Lord Jesus. The multitude was deeply moved but not with anger. They were deeply convicted and inquired of the Apostles what they must do. Peter's reply was, "Repent, and be baptized every one of you in the name of Jesus Christ for the remission of sins, and ye shall receive the gift of the Holy Ghost" (Acts 2:38).

Peter's reply set forth the basic steps necessary for receiving the experience of the salvation provided by the Lord Jesus. These steps had been established by the Lord in His Jordan River experiences. It was the expectation and practice that the new convert should receive the Holy Spirit immediately after their baptism. There were in this transition period some exceptions but the exceptions do not alter the general rule.

Paul was following the general rule and practice in the case of the Ephesian church (Acts 19:1-7). These people were followers of John the Baptist. Paul baptized them in the name of Christ. He then placed his hands on them and they received the gift of the Holy Ghost.

There need not be a dangerous, debilitating delay between conversion and the reception of the Holy Ghost. Why not hold up the experience of the Lord Jesus Christ as our example and pattern to follow? He was baptized by John the Baptist in the Jordan River. A few minutes later, as He stood on the bank of the river praying, John saw the Holy Spirit descend upon Him. What a blessing it would be if sinners could be conditioned to expect to follow this same pattern! No more wilderness road and no more struggles with carnality!! It would seem to be worth a try to bring about this expectation in the minds of the unsaved!!!

CHAPTER 8

Repentance

In contemplating entrance into the salvation provided by the Lord Jesus, we must begin with the ministry of John the Baptist. John's special message was a call to repentance. His was a rugged and demanding call to turn from a sinful life.

This call included all people. It included the religious leaders, the top government officials, the military, and people of all walks of life. A claim to be a descendant of Abraham was not sufficient. All were called to repentance.

It is clear that John the Baptist knew that he was the one that was responsible for preparing the way for the coming of the Lord. His answer to those that inquired about his position and authority was to quote a Messianic prophecy from Isaiah. "He said, I am the voice of one crying in the wilderness, make straight the way of the Lord" (John 1:23). This brings to mind a familiar scene in ancient times. When the king planned to visit a community in his realm, a messenger was sent ahead to announce the king's coming. The people along the route would get busy and repair the roads in their area. They made it as straight as possible. Bumps were removed and chuck holes filled. Stones and all obstructions were removed. They desired to make traveling in their community pleasant for their king. John the Baptist was not thinking about making traveling pleasant for the Lord. It was his purpose to prepare the people's hearts and minds to receive the Lord's message of repentance and His call to the baptism of the Holy Spirit (Matt. 3:11-12).

Jesus did call for repentance. He gave no alternatives. He said, "I tell you nay; but except ye repent, ye shall all likewise perish" (Luke 13:3, 5). John the Baptist's call to repentance and the Lord's call to repentance were in perfect harmony. A strong and a sustained effort must be made to present a clear scriptural understanding of repentance.

Several factors are involved in a genuine repentance. (1) There must be an acknowledgement that known sins have been committed. No excuses are accepted. (2) The proper attitude of repentance is one of deep sorrow and remorse. This includes first of all, the confessing of rebellion against God as manifested in the willful violation of God's commandments. Man seldom reflects upon what a fearful thing it is to deliberately violate a commandment of the almighty God that inhabits eternity. It is a great wickedness to violate the laws of earthly governments, but to willfully violate the laws of the eternal all-powerful Ruler of the universe is sheer madness. It is safer to take on a tornado on a wrestling match than it is to violate with impunity the laws of the Sovereign of all creation.

Man sins not only against God, but also against his fellowman. There is no way to calculate the cost of sin to human society. Think of what we call our justice system. Society has developed elaborate systems to deter criminal (sinful) acts. Complicated lists of unlawful acts are established. Enforcement of these laws requires an extensive police force. When violations occur, it is the duty of the police to apprehend the guilty. A complicated system of courts has been developed to examine the criminal and to pass a proper sentence. To punish criminals it has become necessary to develop a huge system of institutions to administer the punishment the courts have judged proper for the crime committed.

The intangible cost of lawlessness (sin) is quite beyond anything we can imagine or think. There is no way to properly evaluate the awful horror and suffering of the criminal's victims. This suffering would include not only the physical suffering but also the mental anguish resulting from such activity. Also included would be the anguish and suffering of close relatives of the victims.

A sinner should be aware of the awful consequences of sin. This must be a basic factor in repentance. There should be deep sorrow for having engaged in such unrighteous deeds. Evil in the heart is not always expressed in what we call criminal activity. It may not even be expressed openly. There may be bad attitudes or feelings that are concealed in the heart. These may lead to gossip, etc. Repentance calls for confession of these and a deep determination to turn from them.

The call to repentance is also a call to total surrender and commitment to the Lord Jesus Christ. The sinner must be made clearly aware that God demands more than a verbal admission of rebellion and of sins committed. There must be a resolve to turn from a sinful, selfish life to a life committed and surrendered to the Lord Jesus Christ. Could God be just and justify a sinner on anything less than a total surrender and commitment to the Lord Jesus? This total commitment and surrender cannot be delayed until the second step in the salvation experience. The sinner must be conscious that God's willingness to forgive rests upon his determination to surrender and commit himself to the Lord Jesus Christ.

Preaching should prepare and condition the sinner for seeking the Lord in the above manner. Preaching must do more than convince the sinner that as a sinner he is standing in danger of being eternally lost. The sinner must also be clearly instructed as to the steps necessary to escape the wrath of God. There should be an earnest desire to be reconciled with God. As soon as reconciliation has taken place, the next step is to invite the Holy Spirit to come into the newly swept and garnished house. The abiding presence of the Holy Spirit is absolutely necessary to provide the needed strength, etc., to succeed in the Christian life. The Spirit's presence blocks the return of the evil spirit that had been cast out and He also imparts the strength necessary to live the holy life. His presence sheds abroad in the heart not only the love of God (Rom. 5:5) but also the other fruits of the Spirit (Gal. 5:22).

CHAPTER 9

The New Birth

The Jews, in the Lord's day, were living in the hope of the New Covenant that God had promised through the prophets. They interpreted this New Covenant in terms of the Old Covenant. The kingdom set up under the New Covenant would be far superior to the old one. Their mistake at this point was to think in political and social terms. They did not see that a new kingdom demanded "new" citizens. A kingdom of the same old people would be the same old kingdom that they were familiar with. But God had something far different in mind.

In Ezekiel 36:21-28, we have a brief description of the new citizens that will inhabit the new kingdom. (1) They will be a "called out" people (v. 26). (2) God will sprinkle them with clean water and cleanse them from all their filthiness (v. 25). (3) He will give them a new heart (v. 26). (4) God will give them a new spirit (v. 26). (5) Topping all of this, God promised to put "my Spirit within you" (v. 27). This, in essence represents the "new kingdom"; this is the heart of the New Covenant. No doubt, this is what Jesus had in mind when Nicodemus came to see Him. It is a picture of the "New Birth."

It is extremely important that the Biblical concept of the New Birth be clearly presented. The experiences of the Lord Jesus must be held up as the perfect example of how to enter into this New Birth. It was not necessary for him to be born again, but as the great Teacher, He knew the value of an example.

The baptism of the Lord represents the first step toward the New Birth. Perhaps we should say that baptism represents the culmination of this first step. It is the public testimony or witness of several things. (1) That there has been a genuine repentance, confession of sin, and a turning from worldly ways. (2) Baptism is a public witness that a total commitment to the Lord Jesus Christ has been made. And

(3) that God has heard the sinner's prayer and has graciously forgiven the confessed sins and has by regeneration broken the power of sin and imparted a new spirit and a new life to the redeemed child of God.

No effort should be spared to make these steps clear to the sinner. The quality of their religious experience is influenced by the clarity of their understanding and the determination with which they act. It is important that repentance should be the result of a deliberate, wilful, and intellectual choice and not simply a yielding to the emotional pressure of conviction and guilt.

When conditions are met, there can be no question about whether or not God will act. He saw the Prodigal Son a long way off and ran to meet him. Acceptance and forgiveness are assured. This positive assurance is very important to a strong successful Christian life. There is a double witness at this point. (1) The conscience will witness to the release from guilt and condemnation. (2) The Holy Spirit will witness to the fact that the sinner has indeed become a child of God. The new convert is now, according to New Testament practice, ready to make a public confession of faith in Christ by baptism.

Baptism has been debated from about every conceivable standpoint. Much of it has not contributed a great deal to the spiritual enrichment of the Church. There seemed to be some flexibility in the New Testament practice. Circumstances led to some degree of flexibility. The thief on the cross was accepted into Paradise without baptism. Cornelius and his household were baptized after they were filled with the Holy Spirit. The Ephesian believers (Acts 19:1-6) were re-baptized by the Apostle Paul. No doubt, some of these variations may be charged to this being a transition period. To avoid confusion we must follow the example that the Lord Jesus has set before us.

This first step toward the New Birth is to be born of water. It involves confession, repentance, and a total surrender and commitment to the Lord Jesus Christ. The repenting sinners must completely and totally identify themselves with the Lord Jesus. They must take upon themselves the name of Christ. This is what it means to be born of water.

The second step in the New Birth is to be born of the Spirit. This step is illustrated by what happened while the Lord Jesus was standing on the bank of the river. As He stood there praying, John the Baptist saw the Holy Spirit in the form of a dove descend upon Him. The time between His baptism and the reception of the Spirit was a matter of but a few minutes. What John saw here convinced him that Jesus was indeed the promised Messiah (John 1:32-34).

Our present concern is not so much the manner of the Spirit's coming, but the time of His coming. There is no long delay between the Lord's baptism and His reception of the Holy Spirit. May God help us to follow the example of the Lord Jesus in this great experience! This is a must in every Christian's life.

John Wesley was dead wrong in his notion that God confronted every Christian with this opportunity to travel the higher road, but if they chose not to travel this "higher road" and remained faithful to the end they would be saved. Wesley seemed to be thinking in terms of entire sanctification, or a clean heart. But it is a far more serious matter than that. It is rejecting the abiding presence of the Promised Comforter, the Holy Spirit.

Charles G. Finney was nearer the truth. It was his opinion that converts who did not immediately press on and receive the baptism of the Holy Spirit would inevitably backslide (*Systematiac Theology,* pp. 413-14). Perhaps the Lord's parable about the swept and garnished house applies here (Matt. 12:43-45). The tragedy of this parable is that the house remained empty. Who was expected to occupy the house after the evil spirit had been cast out? The most logical tenant would be the Holy Spirit. Why did not He come in? The Holy Spirit (using Dr. C. W. Butler's expression) "is a perfect gentleman." He would not barge in without an invitation. We are, at this point, face to face with a very basic problem. How can we condition and prepare the sinner so that he will follow the example of the Lord Jesus?

This is the greatest challenge facing the Holiness Movement today. There can never be a better time to seek the gift of the Spirit than immediately after conversion. We encompass heaven and earth to win converts and then allow three-fourths of them to fall away because they do not immediately seek the gift of the Holy Spirit. A large share of this loss is the result of our theology. We are strong believers in a carnal period in every Christian's life. In fact, we depend upon the carnal nature to manifest itself and draw our attention to the need of heart purity. Then we add insult to injury by greatly emphasizing the need of cleansing to the point of reducing the gift of the Holy Spirit to a very secondary role.

In the example of the Lord Jesus there is no room for a carnal period. Some are sure to get things mixed up, but ought we not try to present the Lord's example so clearly and powerfully that repenting sinners will come to the altar expecting to immediately follow the Lord's example and seek the gift of the Holy Ghost? Remember the swept and garnished house!

In the name of the Father, Son, and the Holy Spirit, let us give the Lord's example a try!!

CHAPTER 10

Pentecost—The Day the Church Caught Fire

The events surrounding the death and resurrection of the Lord Jesus Christ must have had a mighty impact upon the followers of the Lord. His crucifixion filled them with grief, disappointment and despair. Their dreams and high hopes of a prominent place in the coming Kingdom of God were replaced by fear and confusion. They went into hiding behind locked doors because they had no way of knowing how far the wrath of the authorities might extend in their endeavor to suppress the movement begun by the Lord Jesus. Would they be satisfied with the crucifixion of the Lord or would they also seek His followers and destroy them? It was a crucial time for them. Only something supernatural could rescue them from the depths of their fear and despondency.

Reports of the Lord's resurrection began to filter in. These were confused by conflicting claims. The Roman guards at the tomb had been bribed by the authorities to report that the Lord's body had been stolen while they were sleeping. This was a very unlikely story. Roman guards guilty of such dereliction of duty were put to sleep permanently. Herod executed those that were guarding Peter when the angel liberated him from prison (Acts 12:18-19).

The disciples were reluctant to accept the women's report that the Lord had appeared to them. Over a period of forty days the Lord appeared to various ones of the Apostolic group. In one of His appearances to the women, He instructed them to tell Peter and the others to meet Him on a certain mountain in Galilee. It was probably here that He appeared to the five hundred that Paul speaks about in I Cor. 15:6. His last appearance was to the eleven and others in Jerusalem. He led them from the city as far as Bethany. During this time He gave them a final command. "And, behold, I send the promise of my Father upon you: but tarry ye in the city of Jerusalem, until ye be endued with power from on high" (Luke 24:49). His final act was to lift His hands and bless them. As He did this, He was lifted up from the earth "and a cloud received him out of their sight" (Acts 1:9). "And they worshiped him, and returned to Jerusalem with great joy" (Luke 24:52).

Among the Lord's last words to the Apostles was a command not to "Depart from Jerusalem, but wait for the promise of the Father, which, saith he, ye have heard of me. For John truly baptized with water, but ye shall be baptized with the Holy Ghost not many days hence" (Acts 1:4-5). It is not likely that they understood very well what it meant to be baptized with the Holy Ghost, but they had learned to obey the Lord's commands. They did have before them the testimony of John the Baptist. He had seen the Holy Spirit descend upon the Lord (Matt. 3:16). God had given to John this sign to indicate the One that would baptize with the Holy Ghost. For John, this was proof that Jesus was the Son of God (John 1:29-34).

When they returned to Jerusalem, they went into an upstairs room where they were staying. This could have been the upper room where they had eaten the Last Supper with the Lord Jesus. It would seem natural for them to seek a room that was familiar to them. The danger that had threatened at the time of the crucifixion had subsided. Forty days had gone by since that event. This allowed them to move more freely in the city and in the temple area.

Their chief occupation at the Temple was to offer up prayers and supplications (Acts 1:14). This prayer group included "the women, and Mary the mother of Jesus and with his brethren," along with many other followers. The total number of the group was "about one hundred and twenty" (Acts 1:15). They usually met in Solomon's porch (Acts 5:12). This was one of several small colonnade structures in the Temple area. Some say that Solomon's porch was one of the structures that survived the destruction of Solomon's Temple. These small structures were for the convenience of small group meetings at the Temple. The disciples were familiar with Solomon's Porch. John records the fact that Jesus walked there (John 10:23). Peter and John were on their way to Solomon's Porch when they healed the cripple at the gate Beautiful. This act of healing created considerable excitement among the worshipers at the temple. "All the people ran together unto them in the porch that is called Solomon's, greatly wondering" (Acts 3:11). The ten days following the Lord's ascension were spent here in prayer.

Pentecost was one of the more important Jewish feast days. The Temple court was filled with worshipers. Estimates of the number of worshipers range from one hundred thousand to around three million. Regardless, it was an exciting time and religious fervor was at a high level. Suddenly, this intense religious activity was interrupted by the roar of a mighty rushing wind coming down out of heaven. It focused upon Solomon's Porch. All eyes were fixed upon the colonnade. Those close by, no doubt, saw the cloven tongues of fire that came to rest upon those that were within the colonnade.

The response of those that witnessed these manifestations was swift. The spectators rushed over to the colonnade and the disciples in the colonnade came rushing out. Considerable talking must have taken place. Perhaps each of the one hundred and twenty gathered a small group and preached to them. Or it may have been just the Apostles that spoke. The thing that astonished the crowd was that they heard these Galileans speaking in their own native language. The Bible lists a dozen or more language groups represented in the crowd. Was the miracle in the tongues of the speakers or in the ears of the listeners? When Peter stood up and took charge, there was only one speaker, and he no doubt spoke in the Galilean tongue. There is no indication that many of those present could not understand him. The response of the crowd would seem to indicate that they did understand him. Peter could not have spoken in a dozen languages at the same time. This would seem to indicate that the miracle was in the hearing of the listeners. However we may look at it, the real miracle of Pentecost was not the solution of the language problem, but what had happened to the disciples.

The Church had indeed caught fire. Like Samson's foxes, they scattered the fire of the Spirit wherever they went. The membership of the church leaped from 120 to 3,000 on that day of Pentecost (Acts 2:4). In a few days the membership reached close to 5,000 (Acts 4:4). Nothing can stimulate church growth so well as the anointing fire of the Holy Spirit.

The New Testament church cannot be understood apart from the Pentecostal experience. The indwelling Spirit was a powerful emotional motivating factor that transcended human resources. Peter's statement to the council illustrates this fact. He said, "We cannot but speak the things which we have seen and heard" (Acts 4:20). Threats of punishment and death could not deter them from proclaiming the Gospel. No doubt many accepted the Gospel because they desired the dynamic experience that they saw manifested in the lives of the Apostles.

Careful attention should be given to the New Testament religious experience. They seemed to follow the pattern and example set by the Lord in His initial experiences at the Jordan River. Their usual practice was to baptize the new convert and then place their hands upon them and pray for them to be filled with the Spirit. This is clearly demonstrated by Paul in his ministry to the Ephesians (Acts 19:1-6).

There are variations from this pattern in the New Testament. Cornelius seems to be a variation from the Lord's example. He received the Holy Spirit before he was baptized. The Scriptures indicate that he was a godly man and accepted of God. This would seem to indicate that he was a candidate for the baptism of the Spirit and not for conversion and baptism. Philip's experience in Samaria would seem to indicate that he may have believed that only the Apostles had the power to lay on hands for the reception of the Spirit.

These variations do not disprove the contention that Christian experience should follow the example set before us by the Lord Jesus in His Jordan River experiences. Variations may indeed occur but there must be a basic pattern established to avoid confusion. There is a real danger of an individual becoming confused by the varied theologies of Christian experience. We have a strong tendency to feel that our own experience illustrates the steps that must be followed. The Calvinists contend that the Holy Spirit is received in the initial conversion experience. Those of the Wesleyan persuasion teach that the baptism of the Spirit is received as a very distinct experience subsequent to the initial conversion experience.

At first Wesley, on the basis of observation, believed that the experience came shortly, perhaps a year, before death.

He later became convinced that it was possible to receive it much earlier than that. Soon he urged his ministers to encourage the new convert to immediately begin seeking this experience. There has developed a tendency to accept a lengthy period between conversion and receiving the Holy Spirit. Left to human initiative and example, the wilderness road has become a fact of Christian experience. It has been a disaster for the cause of Christ. The great majority on that road are swallowed up in the wilderness and never make it to the promised land.

Our only hope of escaping disaster is to follow the example of the Lord Jesus Christ. He was baptized by John the Baptist in the river Jordan. A few minutes later as He prayed on the bank of the river, the Holy Spirit descended upon Him. This is the example that we should forever hold before the people. Preaching should condition people to expect to follow this example of the Lord Jesus Christ.

It is a horrendous mistake to encourage the new convert to wait until they discover their carnal condition and the Holy Spirit convicts them of the need of a clean heart. The discovery of carnality indicates that the "evil spirit" has moved back into his old home. That soul is already pretty far down the drain.

It is well to keep in mind that the gift of the Holy Spirit also represents two things. (1) His presence is God's seal or mark of ownership (Ephesians 4:30). In the final day of redemption God will screen out those that bear this mark and receive them into His presence. (2) God has given the Holy Spirit as a guarantee that when our earthly tent is destroyed that we have a building from God, a house not made with hands, eternal in the heavens (II Corinthians 5:1-5).

CHAPTER 11

The Origin of the Long Delay

The long delay between conversion and receiving the Holy Spirit was not present in the Apostles' presentation of the Gospel, nor was it present in the experience of those that believed on the Lord Jesus Christ through the Apostles' preaching. Peter's sermon on the day of Pentecost indicated that he expected the new converts to receive the Spirit immediately after their believing on the Lord Jesus. Perhaps, after Peter's sermon, the rest of the day was spent in baptizing and instructing the three thousand believers. The Holy Spirit may have fallen upon them as He later came upon the household of Cornelius. Certainly, their manner of living indicates that something had happened to them. The Scripture states that, "They devoted themselves to the apostles' teaching and to the fellowship, to the breaking of bread and to prayer" (Acts 2:42).

There seemed to be no problem in getting the new converts to seek the gift of the Holy Spirit. Reception of the Spirit was a most remarkable experience and no doubt was a factor in leading many to believe on the Lord Jesus. They wanted to experience for themselves what the Apostles had experienced on the day of Pentecost.

It would be naive to suppose that all believers in the New Testament went on immediately to their Pentecost. No doubt some failed to seek the gift of the Spirit and some went through the ritual but failed to receive the Holy Spirit. Others may have received the Spirit but soon grieved Him from their hearts. The New Testament Church had its Ananias and Sapphira and the wilderness road Christians of the Corinthian Church.

One of the amazing things in Church History is how quickly the Church lost sight of Pentecost as a personal experience. It continued to observe a Day of Pentecost during the church year but the thrust of the original Pentecost was missing in the lives of the people. The Gentile church soon became thoroughly ritualized. By the time of Constantine (313-337 A.D.), the Church had become so thoroughly ritualized that he could have his armies baptized en masse and brought into the Church. He made Christianity the state religion of the Empire. This was a great victory for the Church but the cost to the Church was high. This attempt to Christianize the pagan empire en masse brought into the Church a flood of paganism that practically obliterated primitive Christianity. The main body of the Church has never recovered from this baptism of paganism.

Primitive Christianity has been kept alive by the formation of new denominations. Those that become disenchanted with the older denominations and desire to recover the New Testament spirit usually follow this procedure. This is not to say that all Church divisions are beneficial and to be encouraged. Certainly some have been harmful. We do, however, have to face the fact that it is extremely difficult to reform an organization from the inside.

John Wesley was a member of the Anglican Church which was cold and formal. He was strongly influenced by two dissenting groups, Puritans and the Moravians. These groups advocated a personal experience of salvation. This was what Wesley was seeking. The tragedy is that he did not leave a clear account of the steps that led him to his goal. He preached two definite works of Grace. When did he experience these two works?

It appears likely that the first step occurred in 1725 when he was twenty-three years old. He wrote, "In 1725 I met with Bishop Taylor's 'Rules of Holy Living and Dying.' I was struck particularly with the chapter upon 'intention,' and felt a fixed intention 'to give myself up to God.' In this I was much confirmed soon after by the 'Christian Pattern' (Thomas a Kempis), and I longed to give to God all my heart. This is what I mean by Christian perfection now" (*Journal,* May, 1765).

Wesley pressed on in his search for Christian Perfection. He was an extremely busy, hard-working man. His activities even led him to spend two years in Georgia. He soon discovered that the New World did not satisfy the deep longing of his heart. After his return to England, he sought Peter Bohler, a Moravian leader, and consulted him about his spiritual problems. On May 24, 1738, he experienced a troubled evening. He desired to remain at his lodging and retire alone "that God might find me." Instead of this, he went reluctantly to a meeting at a Society in Aldersgate Street. Here he listened to someone reading from the preface of Luther's commentary on the Epistle of the Romans. Before Wesley could raise his usual questions something happened. He said, "I felt my heart strangely warmed. I felt I did trust in Christ, Christ alone for my salvation; and an assurance was given me that he had taken away my sins, even mine, and saved me from the law of sin and death" (*John Wesley, His Life and Theology*, Tuttle, pp. 194-5.

Aldersgate came thirteen years after his conversion experience in 1725. He had survived his wilderness road wanderings. His experience led him to entertain some notions that were not helpful. Observations led him to believe that this experience of entire sanctification was usually not obtained until about a year or so before death. He went so far as to claim that this opportunity to walk the higher road is offered to every Christian some time during their life. If they chose not to accept it and remained faithful to their justified state to the end, they would be saved. At its best this appears to be highly risky. Charles G. Finney said that his observations led him to believe that if the new convert failed to immediately press on and receive the baptism of the Spirit they inevitably backslid. Finney's suggestion seems to be the correct position.

Wesley's own Christian experience was a strong factor in the acceptance of a long period of time between conversion and the reception of the Holy Spirit. This position was strengthened by his inquiries into the experiences of hundreds and even thousands of others that claimed to have had the experience of entire sanctification. The great majority of those professing the experience testified that they had received this experience months and even years after their conversion. Some testified that they had received this experience a week or two after their conversion. Wesley seemed astonished when a very small number testified that only a day or two after their conversion, they had received this experience. The preponderance of evidence was on the side of the long delay.

From the spiritual standpoint, delay is always dangerous if not a disaster. There should be no second crisis in the Christian's experience. Instead, it should be a matter of eager expectation, and joyful anticipation of receiving the Holy Spirit. In man's present state no greater privilege can be offered to him than this. Think what it means! God, in the person of the Holy Spirit dwelling in the heart, walking and fellowshipping with man. How can one remain in touch with God and delay or refuse such an offer?

A part of the problem is the overemphasis upon cleansing or entire sanctification. One can read page after page of holiness literature that extols the experience of entire sanctification but little is said about the indwelling presence of the Holy Spirit. He is definitely relegated to a secondary place. Cleansing is the big thing. This is not as it should be.

The Lord's parable about the swept and garnished house helps to clarify the situation (Luke 11:24-26). We have here a picture of a person that had taken the first step in the salvation experience but failed to invite the Holy Spirit in immediately after that first step. The house had been cleansed and put in order for the New Occupant but He did not come in because He had not been invited. Dr. C. W. Butler characterized the Holy Spirit as a perfect gentleman. He must be invited to make the human heart His abode. He will not rudely move in and take over without a sincere invitation to come into the newly cleansed temple.

There should be no second "crisis" in the Christian experience. It should be a joyful transition from being a purged empty house to one occupied by the Divine Guest. Delay plays havoc with God's perfect plan of salvation. Failure to invite the Comforter in immediately leads to defeat and confusion. The former evil occupant moves back in and brings several fellow spirits with him. The final state of that man is worse than the first (Luke 11:26). Every effort should be made to avoid this tragedy.

Late in life John Wesley lamented, "I have been lately thinking a good deal on one point wherein, perhaps, we have all been wanting. We have not made it a rule, as soon as ever a person is justified, to remind them of going on to perfection! Whereas it is the very time preferable to all others. They have then the simplicity of children; and they are fervent in spirit, and ready to cut off a right hand or pluck out the right eye. But if we once suffer this fervor to subside, we shall find it hard enough to bring them again even to this point" (Letter to Thomas Rankin). John Wesley did not solve this problem nor have his followers solved it.

A prominent factor in the development of the long delay between the two steps of the salvation experience was the strong tendency to follow actual experience. Wesley himself experienced at least a six to a thirteen year delay in his own experience. Wesley was not at all clear about his own experience. Some believe he was converted in 1725 and filled with the Spirit at Aldersgate. Others believe that he was converted at Aldersgate and experienced the second work sometime around 1744.

Wesley was quite pragmatic. He personally examined literally hundreds and thousands of his followers as to the steps in their religious experience. He found that a long delay between justification and entire sanctification was the usual pattern. In spite of his later insights he was never able to change that pattern.

The modern Holiness Movement must make a determined effort to rid itself of this unscriptural, dangerous, and disastrous delay. We are confusing our people by a heavy dependence upon human experience. Our motto must be, "Looking unto Jesus the author and finisher of our faith." He set before us in His Jordan River experience the necessary steps to receive the salvation that He died to provide. Only a few minutes separated these experiences. These cannot be compressed into one experience, nor should a long period of time between them be encouraged. Sometimes the new convert is encouraged to go out and live for the Lord until the carnal nature manifests itself and God convicts him of the need of a clean heart, then he is urged to seek entire sanctification. This is confusing. We are not, at this point, dealing with a carnal nature that remains after conversion, but with an evil spirit that had been cast out at conversion, and now has moved back into his former home. This confusion accounts for many of the poor examples of the holiness life among our holiness people.

The remedy of this situation is to follow the example of the Lord Jesus. There must be a genuine repentance and a turning from sin. When assurance of forgiveness has been received, the new convert should seek immediately the gift of the Holy Spirit. The house is swept and garnished, ready to receive the new Occupant. Any departure from the Lord's example leads to confusion and disaster. The big question facing theology today is not how to get back to Luther, Calvin, or Wesley, but how to get back to the Lord Jesus Christ and to the examples He set before us. It is impossible to think of a better way to bring to this world what is needed to cure the evils of men, and thus make it possible to develop a truly just and fair society.

References

1. Bloesch, Donald, *The Ground of Certainty* (Grand Rapids: William B. Eerdmans Publishing Company).

2. Finney, Charles, *Finney's Systematic Theology* (Minneapolis: Bethany Fellowship Inc.).

3. James, William, *The Will to Believe* (New York: Longmans, Green and Co.).

4. Keen, S. A., *Faith Papers*.

5. Peirce, Charles S., Edited, with an Introduction and Notes by Philip P. Wiener, *Selected Writings* (Values in a Universe of Change) (New York: Dover Publications, Inc.).

6. Randall, *The Making of the Modern Mind.*

7. Tuttle, Robert G., Jr., *John Wesley His Life and Theology* (Grand Rapids: Zondervan Publishing House).